RAILROAD STATIONS
OF DELMARVA
THROUGH TIME

DOUGLAS POORE

AMERICA
THROUGH TIME®
ADDING COLOR TO AMERICAN HISTORY

America Through Time is an imprint of Fonthill Media LLC
www.through-time.com
office@through-time.com

Published by Arcadia Publishing by arrangement with Fonthill Media LLC
For all general information, please contact Arcadia Publishing:
Telephone: 843-853-2070
Fax: 843-853-0044
E-mail: sales@arcadiapublishing.com
For customer service and orders:
Toll-Free 1-888-313-2665

www.arcadiapublishing.com

First published 2021

Copyright © Douglas Poore 2021

ISBN 978-1-63499-372-2

Typeset in Mrs Eaves XL Serif Narrow
Printed and bound in England

CONTENTS

ACKNOWLEDGMENTS

To each and every person I have met on this incredible three-year journey of research, thank you all for your encouragement, stories, photos, and so much more. Each of you have helped to create these books. I am just the person who has had the honor of putting pen to paper.

To my family, words cannot begin to convey how I feel about all the love and support through all of this. Shew, what an endeavor.

To everyone at Fonthill Media, thank you for believing in my crazy train idea.

To all the museums, historical societies, Facebook group members, and anyone else that provided photos for this book: thank you. A special thank you to the Greater Harrington Historical Society. Any photo not marked is courtesy of this organization.

To the family of Ed Sharpe, your father was a great man. We lost a wonderful railroad mind this year.

Finally, to all that read this book, thumb through it pages. The train was always a way to get from here to there. Just be sure to always leave a candle lit in the window to light your way home.

INTRODUCTION

Since its birth, owed to early stations for ships, these railroad station buildings served a purpose that went far beyond their intent, which was simply to be a place to board a train from here to there. Writing the third book of the series on the railroads of Delmarva, I struggled at first on exactly how to present the information. I mean, after all, one can only talk so much about a building. Walls, windows, doors, and floors spark the imagination for some, but when so many of these buildings on Delmarva were cookie-cutter designed, after a while, the words would be a drumbeat that was seemingly never-ending. Then, as I thought, I realized what made these buildings special were the stories behind them, the people that worked in them, the towns they sat in, and the events that would play out inside of these four walls.

As I explored this approach, my mind began to recall the images and scenes that have become so familiar to so many over the centuries. The first commercially produced movie was that of a railroad station, *Arrival of a Train*, produced in France in 1895. This fifty-second silent film shows the entry of a train pulled by a steam locomotive into a train station at the French coastal town of La Ciotat. There is an urban legend associated with this movie that says when the film was first shown, the audience was so scared by the image of a life-sized train barreling toward them that people screamed and ran to the back of the room.

To date, there are over 500 films that have used trains or railroad stations as their focus or backdrop. Perhaps the most recognizable today due to its tremendous fan base is Kings Cross Station in England with Platform 9 ¾. Of course, I am referring to the *Harry Potter* books. These scenes have become so famous that they have placed a baggage cart in the wall at the station so fans can take their picture and recreate those iconic moments.

Television has also used the railroad station has a backdrop. If you are the age of this author, you will remember three beautiful women skinny-dipping in the water tank at *Petticoat Junction*, a sitcom in the late 1960s on C.B.S. This show, more than any other, portrayed life in a small town and how the railroad station became not just a place but a destination all its own.

Railroad stations, and we will get into the name debate shortly, are unique structures. Big or small, serving many platforms or a single rail line all had one thing in common: they had two main entrances—one entrance facing the community and the other facing the train tracks themselves. Some were huge structures with restaurants, hotels, shops, and offices housed within while some were no more than sheds. They could be on the street level, high up on a platform, or below ground. Some even served as both passenger stations and depot stations combined.

What to call these structures has even been debated. The term "train station" is generally described as the physical building where passengers boarded and departed from their train. However, the railroad defined a "station" as a stopping point that may, or may not, contain a building. These locations could feature anything from a water tank to a siding or simply a sign. The "depot" was the term regularly reserved for small facilities while "terminal" often described the very large structures. There was also the term "union station," detailing those buildings used or shared by at least two or more railroads, a few of which existed on Delmarva. For the purposes of the book, I will keep to the accepted term of "railroad station."

To truly understand the complexities of the railroad station, one must forget the modern thoughts of today. You must harken back to a time before booking online, before travel agents, before FedEx and U.P.S., before news flashed across your phone, and even before the telephone itself. In the 1830s, travel consisted of mostly by foot or by horsepower. Wagons carried goods to market. If they were to be transported great distances, goods went to shipping terminals. Some 90 percent of America lived within a few miles of a waterway during the 1800s and mostly on farms. Most citizens had never traveled more than a few miles from their homes. Our power, industry, and transportation were all based around the movement of water. Yet in 1830, that was all about to change. The initial portion of the Baltimore and Ohio Railroad had reached its first stop, Ellicott Mills, Maryland, a mere 13 miles from its main station in Baltimore and a blink today, but in 1830, that made a day-long trip now only one hour long. Delmarva saw its first train in 1832 on the New Castle and Frenchtown Rail Road, a line from the port at New Castle, Delaware, to another river port located in Frenchtown, Maryland, near Elkton, Maryland today.

After the Civil War and the importance that the railroads displayed in moving people and goods, the railroad came to dominate America, spurring the Industrial Revolution and completely transforming the country. No longer were we a society living on farms; cities grew and grew. Goods could be shipped anywhere in the United States in days, even hours, instead of weeks. Also, the railroad station grew to symbolize America's love affair with the iron horse. Towns grew from nothing but a stop for the train.

Towns moved, abandoning already established sites, just to be located on the rails. Major cities today such as Chicago grew from small populations to the places they are today, all thanks to the railroads. Famous architects were hired, men like Frank Furness who designed both stations that were located in Wilmington Delaware, the firm of Mead, McKim and White, designers of Pennsylvania station in downtown Manhattan.

The smaller stations were commonly designed as multipurpose facilities, and this plan would be used over and over to replicate stations quickly and cheaply.

The railroads and their stations continued to dominate cities and towns alike until after World War One and the appearance of the automobile. Slowly, the transition began away from the railroads and to the car. Smaller stations would see less traffic and would slowly be abandoned or reused for other purposes. With World War Two, the railroad stations reached their busiest peak ever, as our nation moved men and materials in record numbers to win the war. Following this zenith, the decline was rapid. Even larger stations began to show their decay and lack of maintenance as revenues fell sharply. From a peak of 80,000 just prior to World War One, today fewer than 1,000 passenger railroad stations are in use, excluding commuter subway stations.

Delmarva had a known total of 386 railroad stations, post stops, and flag stops. To date, some 150 structures have been found and photographed, most of them finding a home in these pages.

Today, many of the iconic stations such as the Pennsylvania station in downtown Manhattan are gone, victims of the wrecking ball. Smaller stations too have been destroyed or left to rot in place until they collapsed under their own weight. Others thankfully have seen a rebirth as office space, restaurants, museums, or government buildings. Within these pages, we will journey back to the time when the railroad station was more than just a place for a person to catch a train and show you how that building survives today. So, grab your ticket and "all aboard."

1

PHILADELPHIA, WILMINGTON, AND BALTIMORE RAILROAD

The Philadelphia, Wilmington, and Baltimore Railroad (P.W.&B.) was born out of four railroads, all of which were created by their respective state legislators in 1831. For the readers that do not know, railroads are incorporated by each state, so for lines to travel intrastate, connecting lines had to be established. The four railroads were owned by the Philadelphia and Delaware County Rail-Road Company; Wilmington and Susquehanna Rail Road Company; Baltimore and Port Deposit Rail Road Company; and the Delaware and Maryland Rail Road Company. This railroad, however, was not the first to traverse Delmarva. Constructed two years earlier, the New Castle and Frenchtown Rail Road traveled from New Castle, Delaware, to Frenchtown, Maryland, but no railroad stations were ever constructed on this line.

When the P.W.&B. began operations, only four stations were originally constructed. None of those original stations exist today. After purchasing the New Castle and Frenchtown Rail Road in 1839, the P.W.&B. set out to expand, and by 1890, it now had twelve stops in Delaware. The Newark station was constructed in 1877. The interior of the two-floor building featured separate waiting rooms for men and women, an office and baggage room, kitchen cellar, bedrooms, and a sitting room. The station developed into a main center of activity due to its important location at the junctions of the P.W.&B.'s line with both the Delaware Railroad and the Pomeroy branch of the Pennsylvania Railroad. In 1988, the building was restored and today serves as a historical museum. (*Top: Courtesy Keith Short; bottom: Courtesy Kevin Painter*)

Newport railroad station was a constructed in about 1908, again replacing an earlier structure. It was a one-story frame building in the Bungalow/American Craftsman style. The station was closed to passenger traffic in the late 1940s. The station was then left to slowly deteriorate and was eventually demolished in the late 1990s despite being placed on the National Register of Historic Places in 1994. Today, you can still see the stairs that lead from the station level to the street level below. (*Top: Courtesy of Hagley Museum; bottom: Courtesy Keith Short*)

The P. B. & W. Railroad Depot,
Front and French Sts., Wilmington, Del.

Wilmington was a major connection and a prize location for the P.W.&B. At first, a small wooden structure had been built but in 1907, the Pennsylvania Railroad, which had taken over operations on the P.W.&B., needed a regional headquarters. Renowned architect Frank Furness was commissioned to design the structure. Today, this station, out of the approximately 180 that Furness designed, is one of only eighteen that survive. Two restoration projects—one in 1983 and the second in 2009—have restored this building to its beautiful original design. Placed on the National Registry of Historic Places on July 6, 1976, the building has been renamed in honor of President Joe Biden. Today, the structure serves both Septa and Amtrak along the busy Northeast Corridor. (*Bottom: Courtesy of Amtrak Corporation*)

The most northern railroad station to call Delaware home on the P.W.&B. line was Claymont, Delaware. The oldest station was built in the 1870s, then replaced in the early twentieth century. This station served until it was destroyed by an arson fire on July 25, 1981. Since Septa was the only line now servicing this station, just a small covering was constructed to serve the passengers. However, that is not the end of the story. Beginning as early as 2005, plans were under way for a regional transportation center. Slated to open in the fall of 2021, the Claymont Regional Transportation Center, a $74-million project, will include a railroad station, shops, homes, offices, and warehouse space. (*Top: Courtesy of Delaware Public Archives; bottom: Courtesy of Delaware Department of Transportation*)

2

THE DELAWARE RAILROAD

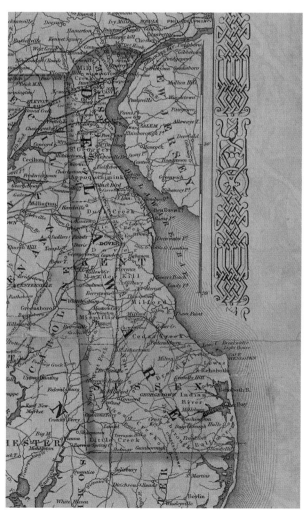

The Delaware Railroad was the first railroad to travel north and south on the Delmarva Peninsula and follows that same line even today. Originally charted on June 20, 1836, it took the foresight of Judge Samuel Harrington to champion the railroad and help secure funding. Construction began in 1852 with backing already from the P.W.&B. The line reached the state capital of Dover in 1855 and Seaford by the winter of 1856. The first section was opened with an inaugural eight-car train north from Middletown on September 1, 1855, carrying the president of the railroad and that of the New Castle and Frenchtown Railroad, the chief engineer, and railroad contractors. Only two of the original stations that were constructed exist today. (*Courtesy of Maryland State Archives*)

Kirkwood, Delaware, was named for Robert Kirkwood, a soldier who fought in the American Revolutionary War. The area was also known as Saint Georges station, which is listed on several different railroad schedules throughout the late 1800s. Robert Kirkwood was a lieutenant serving in multiple battles under General Washington. On August 16, 1780, at the Battle of Camden, Kirkwood's troops fought valiantly and earned the nickname "The Blue Hen's Chickens," which would lead to the Delaware Blue Hen become Delaware's state bird. His college *alma mater*, Newark Academy (later changing its name to the University of Delaware), adopted the blue hen as its mascot in his honor. The station existed until the early 1980s when it was torn down.

Growing from only nineteen stations (mostly barns and sheds in the beginning), the Delaware Railroad grew to thirty-three stops by 1890. By this time, almost all the old stations had been replaced with more modern structures. Today, only ten of these stations exist, none in New Castle County. The first station preserved sits in Clayton, Delaware, a town named after the man that first charted the Delaware Railroad, John M. Clayton in 1835. The brick station was constructed in 1855 and served as a passenger station till service all but ceased in the 1950s. Today, the station is a rental venue for public events. (*Top: Courtesy of Delaware Public Archives*)

From 1885 through 1920, Clayton was division headquarters for the Philadelphia, Wilmington, and Baltimore Railroad. Even though the line still operated as the Delaware Railroad, the line was leased to the P.W.&B. in 1857, and they maintained full financial control over the line. The result was scheduling that connected the Delaware Railroad with other lines under the P. W.&B. control. Using Clayton as a regional office in the building shown here, the line flourished. In 1875, the railroad shipped over 900,000 baskets of peaches, with a crop so large several farmers lost their produce due to a lack of railcars. While passenger service ended, the line even in the 1960s saw multiple freight trains a day. (*Top: Courtesy of Keith Short and Jim Bowden*)

The station in Dover, Delaware, is the second to be built at this location. Dover was the original charter point of the Delaware Railroad. A ferry service had connected Dona Landing, just east of Dover, to Philadelphia. The first act of the Delaware Railroad was to purchase this and quickly close the service once the trains began to run. Constructed in 1911, this federal-style building was a major passenger and shipping location, serving as such until 1965. Used by the justice of the peace as a courthouse, the structure received a renovation in 2001. Today, the structure—named in honor of George V. Massey, the nineteenth-century Dover attorney who convinced the Pennsylvania Railroad to build the station—is used by the state of Delaware. (*Top: Courtesy of Delaware Public Archives*)

Wyoming, Delaware, is a town that really should have never existed. The station and two homes were all that were there when the first agent arrived for the railroad. The reason the station was not placed in nearby Camden was simple—soot. The citizens of Camden did not want the smoke and soot that came with the trains in their town. So, the railroad simply went to the west and built a new town. "Camden Station" or "West Camden" as it was called grew, and in 1865, Reverend John J. Pierce of the Wyoming Valley in Pennsylvania came to "West Camden" and laid it out in building lots. In this same year, it was decided by the citizens of "West Camden" to change the name of their village to Wyoming out of deference to Reverend Pierce. (*Top: Courtesy of Delaware Public Archives*)

Woodside, Delaware, is just one of many towns on Delmarva that came into existence due to the coming of the railroad. Local landowner Henry Cowgill was the force that prompted the Delaware Railroad to establish a depot and station house. The station was first called Willow Grove station, but the name was soon changed to Fredonia by the Cowgill family. The town changed its name on July 2, 1869. Local lore has it that the town received this name because there was a great amount of wood in the form of timber and railroad ties piled on a vacant lot to the side of the station. The original station, constructed in 1864, has now been restored and is in the collection of the Delaware Agricultural Museum. The second station was destroyed after passenger service ended in the 1950s. (*Top: Courtesy of the Delaware Public Archives*)

Another of the Delaware Railroad creations is Felton, Delaware, named after Samuel M. Felton, the then-president of the P.W.&B. The town had no station initially as it was nothing more than a whistle stop that was located at the intersection of two main roadways. The brick station was constructed in the late 1860s and served as a freight and passenger station until the 1950s. The station is owned by the town and currently houses a local museum.

The "Hub of Delaware" was Harrington's nickname for more than 100 years, achieving this moniker from its position on the railroad. This city has served as the end of the line initially, a junction with the aptly named Junction and Breakwater Railroad, and a main switching yard for freight moving north and south even today. While it has gone by many names—such as Clarks Corner or Milford Junction—it was the name "Harrington" that the citizens approved in 1869, to honor Judge Samuel Harrington for his leadership in the railroad industry on Delmarva. Today, the brick station, the second constructed here, serves as home to Delmarva Central Railroad, a subsidiary of Carload Express. The railway is owned by Norfolk Southern and leased to Carload Express, which is based out of Oakmont, PA.

Sitting just south of the main crossing in Harrington is a building that was all too common in the early 1900s along the railroads of Delmarva. Interlocking or block towers were located at busy railyards and junctions, allowing for the operators working these towers to control many switches and signals at once. This not only made operations more streamlined, but reduced errors that could occur with multiple men manually throwing switches and signals in a yard. The tower in Harrington is the only one that exist today as it did in the 1920s. The Greater Harrington Historical Society offers tours of the facility.

Owing its name according to local tales, Greenwood, Delaware, so named for the holly trees that grew in the area, was another whistle stop originally known as Saint Johnstown. The station was constructed in 1858 and today is used as an insurance agency office. On December 2, 1903, during a blinding snowstorm, a southbound train hit another engine that had drifted onto the main line. There was a deafening roar when a boxcar of dynamite exploded, filling the air with flying debris, fire, and smoke. That first blast was followed by another as naphtha tank cars caught fire, spraying burning liquid. The combination of the explosion and the highly flammable liquid spread the intense fire. All but three buildings in the town were damaged. Brakeman Edwin Roach of Georgetown and an infant child died in the tragedy.

Bridgeville, Delaware, was a well-established town by the time the railroad arrived in 1856. The town got its name when a bridge was built over a branch of the Nanticoke River called Bridge Branch, a name that the settlement was also known by. As with all the towns along the railroad, it grew rapidly. Canning factories, produce shipping, and other goods quickly used this newly arrived mode of transportation to move their commodities to the major cities of the northeast. The station continues to serve the food industry today as a storage facility for RAPA Scrapple. (*Top: Courtesy of the Bridgeville Historical Society*)

Seaford, Delaware, was the next station to be the end of the line for the Delaware Railroad. Arriving on December 11, 1856, the railroad head quickly boomed due to the already established steamship landing located adjacent to the end of the line. Multiple seafood packing houses filled railcars to be shipped north. The first railroad station was a box car, that had either been chosen to be used or by some accounts had been wrecked and was just sitting there. The second station was in the "Nanticoke Hotel," constructed in 1869 and later purchased by the Delaware Railroad in June 1875 for $5,125. The final station constructed here was built in 1901 and is still in service today as a yard office for Delmarva Central Railroad. (*Top: Courtesy of Keith Short and Jim Bowden; bottom: Courtesy of Gene Blelie*)

Arriving in 1859, Laurel was yet another small town when the railroad arrived. The town was named for the laurel trees that grew alongside Broad Creek. The original brick station was quickly outgrown, so in 1910, a new larger station with an extended, covered passenger platform was added. The town grew so rapidly that in 1929 the town of North Laurel, which was home to the Broad Creek whistle stop and the main town of Laurel merged. After passenger service ended in the 1950s, the station sat abandoned. Purchased by the town of Laurel, it has been restored and today is home to the Laurel Heritage Museum. (*Top: Courtesy of the Delaware Public Archives*)

3

THE EASTERN SHORE RAILROAD

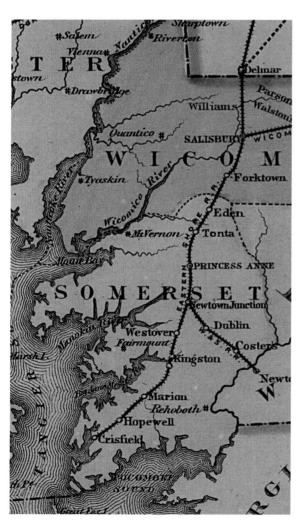

While the Delaware Railroad was in its formative beginnings, another railroad company had its charter revised and began to raise the needed capital to begin construction. The Eastern Shore Railroad had been established in 1833, but funding could not be acquired to construct the line. So, when the Delaware Railroad had to stop at the Maryland–Delaware state line, it needed a connection to bring the bounty of the eastern shore of Maryland to the major cities of the northeast and on into Canada. Plans of the line were now scaled back from its original design, with the connection at the newly created town of Delmar, Delaware, and its terminus being in the busy seafood town of Crisfield, Maryland. (*Courtesy of the Library of Congress, Geography and Map Division*)

Salisbury, Maryland, was a very well-established city by the time the railroad arrived in 1860. Construction of the line was halted due to the Civil War but resumed and was completed to Crisfield, Maryland, in 1866. In 1914, the small shanty station in Salisbury was replaced by a large brick Union station to be used by both the New York, Philadelphia, and New York Railroad, now the owners of the Eastern Shore line and the Baltimore, Chesapeake, and Atlantic Railroad, which traveled east and west. After its closing in 1986 as a railroad facility, the railroad station has been used for a variety of commercial endeavors but today sits abandoned. (*Top: Courtesy of Keith Short and Jim Bowden*)

Founded in 1733, Princess Anne, Maryland, was already a busy port at the head of the Manokin River when the railroad came to call. As with so many original stations, only a small shanty and freight dock were originally constructed. In the late 1880s, a larger brick structure was built to handle the increasing numbers of passengers and the growing seafood trade the line was known for. Not as well-known but almost as popular was the hunting trade that the railroad created in the community. Visitors from all over the east coast would come to the area in the fall to enjoy hunting local game. While the station has been many things since the railroad abandoned the property, the property sits today awaiting its next owners.

4

THE WORCESTER RAILROAD

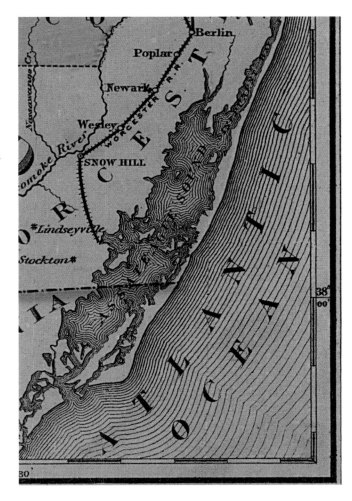

Chartered in 1853, the Worcester Railroad would serve to tie the lower eastern portion of Maryland to the rest of Delmarva. The first section of the line was completed in 1872, connecting Berlin to Snow Hill, Maryland. On April 7, 1876, the line was operational from Selbyville, Delaware, to Franklin City, Virginia. The focus of the line was to tap into the rich seafood industry along the east coast, particularly in Chincoteague, Virginia. The problem facing the small branch line was that there was no town to connect the mainland to the small but rich seafood coast of Chincoteague. That would soon change, and in a big way. (*Courtesy of the Library of Congress, Geography and Map Division*)

We have all heard of a boom to bust town. The greatest example of this phenomenon of the railroads of Delmarva was Franklin City, Virginia. Judge John Rankin Franklin of Maryland owned the swamp at the northeast corner of Virginia. He gave half of it to the railroad to help bring the road across the border to his Virginia property. The boomtown was named Franklin City in his honor. Today, the town is gone, destroyed by hurricanes and time. The area has fewer than fifty inhabitants. The old station has been ordered to be destroyed by the federal government, who owns the property, as it has been undermined by sea water. (*Top: Courtesy of Keith Short and Jim Bowden*)

Family tradition indicates that when Charles W. Bishop, the principal landowner of the area, girdled a large beech tree while clearing land for his home, the area gained its name. First called Girdle Tree Hill and later Girdletree, this small Maryland town saw its fortunes rise and fall with the railroad. By 1900, a bank, cannery, and other businesses had opened as the area flourished. Following the Great Depression, the town has remained stagnant in growth. The small wooden station now sits on city property. The Girdletree Village Historical Foundation has purchased and restored the freight station. They also have a driving tour of historic buildings, which includes the former station master's house. (*Top: Courtesy of Keith Short and Jim Bowden*)

"Snow" is not a word that will first pop into your mind when someone says, "Eastern Shore of Maryland," but nonetheless, Snow Hill, Maryland, has existed since 1686. Named for a district in London, this community was already a busy inland port when the railroad came calling. The first railroad station was constructed in the 1870s and was outgrown by 1900. The later station was constructed of brick and provided office space for the railroad, as well as passenger and freight depots. The city of Snow Hill purchased the station and restored it into a rental space in the 1990s. In 2019, the Maryland and Delaware Railroad returned fright service to the line.

No matter by which name you call it, Newark or Queponco, the small Maryland town has one of the best examples of an early twentieth-century railroad station. The station took the place of a small wooden structure that had first sat on the site. When the new station opened, to distinguish the Newark station from the other railroad stations with the same name in Delaware and New Jersey, the company named the stop, "Queponco Station," taken from the Indian name for the area, said to mean, "the land of the burnt pines." In 1989, the non-profit group, the Queponco Railway Station, Inc., acquired a ninety-nine-year lease for the structure and has restored the building along with creating a small-town museum that highlights local history. (*Bottom: Courtesy of Linda Roy Walls*)

5

THE QUEEN ANNE'S AND KENT RAILROAD

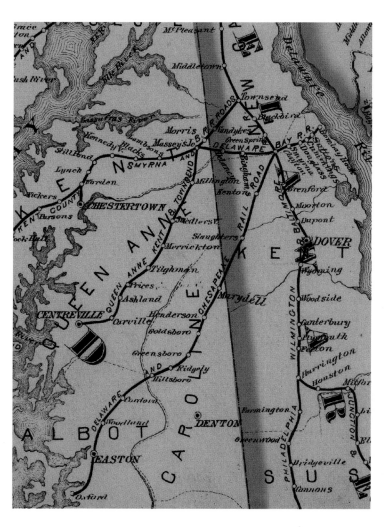

The Queen Anne's and Kent Railroad passed through fourteen stations on its travels from its junction with the Delaware Railroad at Townsend, Delaware, to its end point in Centreville, Maryland. During its late nineteenth and early to mid-twentieth century years of passenger and freight service, it would not be unimaginable that the railroad was in fact the life blood of these communities and nearby farmlands. The Queen Anne's and Kent Railroad traces its origin to an act of the Maryland legislature passed in 1856 to incorporate the Queen Anne's and Kent Railroad. Ground was broken at Millington on January 6, 1868. The contractors began work on May 8, 1868. The lined opened for operation in 1869. (*Courtesy of the Library of Congress, Geography and Map Division*)

The community that was to become Sudlersville took root in 1740 when Joseph Sudler, a Kent Island landowner, purchased 800 acres south of the Chester River. By 1869, the railroad provided transportation not only to those who lived in and around rural Sudlersville, but it also provided a faster means of getting grains and produce to market. By the time a new passenger station was built in 1885, the town had already doubled in size from fifteen to thirty-nine homes. Sudlersville Railroad station remains at its original site. The historic building was purchased in 1987 and restored by the Sudlersville Community Betterment Club. Today, the station houses Jimmy Foxx memorabilia and exhibits that highlight Sudlersville's history. (*Top: Courtesy of Sudlersville Community Betterment Club*)

Barclay, Maryland, is one of the railroad towns that were created by the establishment of the Queen Anne's and Kent Railroad. The line was designed to provide shipping for goods and products from the eastern shore to communities, farmers, and markets in Philadelphia and other cities. In addition, the railroad encouraged the development of communities at rail stops to ensure that there would be natural market points for local products. Within a short time of its creation, the community at Barclay was a small prosperous town with a village core. After the station closed, the building was moved to nearby Sudlersville and has seen several modifications. Today, the structure serves as a home, but you can still see the outline of the original station.

The next station to survive till today has very little history that can be found. Price, Maryland, was created as a stop due to a large country road that crossed the railroad at this point. Since the road allowed for transportation to the station, the village was established, but as with so many small hamlets created by the railroad, citizens followed. Two churches, small stores, and even a post office opened in the area. The rails are still operated, as is this entire line, by the Maryland and Delaware Railroad. The station had been a small home, but today, nature has begun to reclaim the building.

While this book's focus in on the railroad stations that survive today, the reason many of the railroads were built on Delmarva revolved around goods. Be they produce, grains, or seafood, prior to the 1940s, Delmarva was America's capital for most of these commodities. Over 390 railroad stations, whistle stops, and depots were built along these rail lines. The depot in Centerville Maryland is one of the few that exist today. Seen in the background of the postcard, today the depot has been relocated to nearby Bloomfield Farm to be restored as a museum for the Queen Anne's Railroad Society. Sadly, the station is long gone. (*Bottom: Courtesy of Queen Anne's Railroad Society*)

6

THE JUNCTION AND BREAKWATER RAILROAD

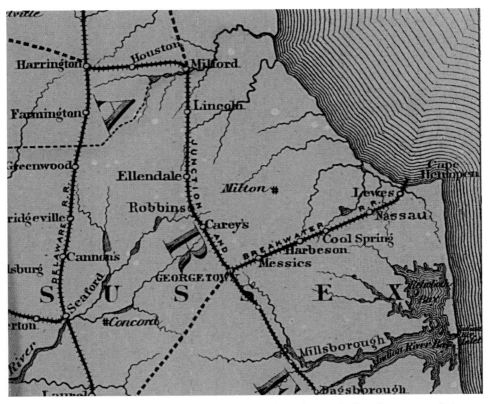

The name says it all for this railroad. The Junction and Breakwater Railroad was to run between the main line of the Delaware Railroad and its yard at Harrington, Delaware, to the breakwater located in Lewes, Delaware. Construction began in 1857 but it was not until January 1, 1870, that the line was opened from start to finish. The lines two major focuses were the inland port of Milford, Delaware, and the vast fishing areas of the Delaware Bay. When completed, the train could back right onto the docks and load freight directly from the sea. (*Courtesy of the Library of Congress, Geography and Map Division*)

The brick station at Milford Delaware was constructed in 1857 and, with few modifications, retains its look from that era. Long known as a deep-water port, no fewer than six shipyards existed prior to the arrival of the railroad. The name Milford came from a dam and mill site that travelers had been using to cross the river—a ford—leading people to call it the mill at the ford, and eventually, the town became known as Milford. A large vocal group lobbied for the Delaware Railroad to take a more easterly tract and come straight to the city, but that effort failed, leaving the city to await the arrival of the train on September 7, 1859.

Georgetown, Delaware, became a center of railroad activity in the late 1800s. Georgetown is named in honor of Commissioner George Mitchell, who was active in the movement to centralize the county seat in the town back in 1791. Always a major railroad junction, no fewer than ten different railroads have crisscrossed the tracks that travel through the center of the town. The station has seen the same changes over that span of time. Constructed in the 1860s, the station had a second story added in 1911, removed after World War Two, added again during its restoration in 2003, severely damaged by fire in 2011, and restored again. This railroad station now serves as a museum and office space. (*Top: Courtesy of the Delaware Public Archives*)

Named for nearby Cool Springs Creek, this area of Sussex County was settled early in the 1700s by a group of Irish immigrants looking to create a community for themselves. A small church and a few houses are all that have ever called this village home. When the Junction and Breakwater Railroad built a small railroad station/depot combination here, the existing road created a unique crossing for both vehicles and trains alike. The restored station sits on private land, with just the passenger portion existing today. (*Top: Courtesy of the Delaware Public Archives*)

Nassau, Delaware, was a stop named by the railroad. No one seems to know exactly where the name comes from. A fort built across the Delaware River in 1627 was called Fort Nassau and was constructed by the Dutch, naming it after the House of Orange-Nassau, the monarchy of the Netherlands. Nearby Lewes was founded by the same explorers, so it is a safe bet that is where the name of this town came from. What is known for sure is why there was a stop placed here—peaches and apples, with the peach count putting Georgia to shame. After the station sat abandoned for decades, the structure was moved to Nassau Vineyards, Delaware's oldest winery. The station has recently been used as the cornerstone of a business office at the winery.

7

THE MARYLAND AND DELAWARE RAILROAD

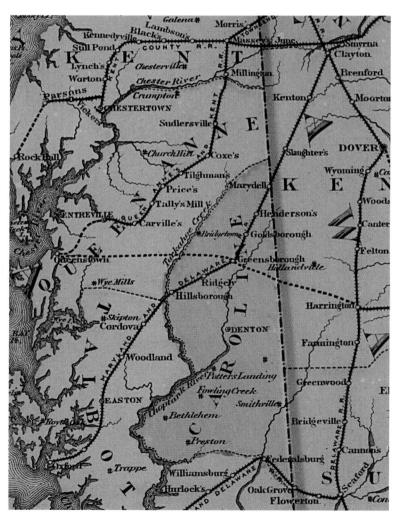

Sometimes, simple is best. That is the rule the next line built on Delmarva followed. Called the Maryland and Delaware Railroad for the two states it covered, this line intersected the Delaware Railroad in Clayton, Delaware, and initially ended in Easton, Maryland. Within a few years, the rails would extend to the town of Oxford, Maryland. Built to serve industry and agriculture, the line was sold into bankruptcy by 1877 and was reorganized as the Delaware and Chesapeake Railroad. Today, only a small, abandoned section of rail, a few decaying bridges, and a handful of railroad stations remain. (*Courtesy of the Library of Congress, Geography and Map Division*)

Originally called Arthursville, this small village was renamed "Hartly" for a Mr. Hart, a railroad employee, who was instrumental in bringing the railroad to the area. The rail line was laid in the 1850s with the first depot located half a mile south of Hartly at Slaughter station. By 1882, Hartly had grown to include a store, a church, a schoolhouse, a post office, several houses, and even a hotel. With this growth, a new station was built to allow for the increase in goods and passengers. Today, the home sits near its original location—a shell of its former beauty. (*Top: Courtesy of the Delaware Public Archives*)

Goldsboro is one of the railroad towns that were created by the establishment of the Maryland and Delaware Railroad. The line was designed to provide shipping for goods and products from the eastern shore to communities, farmers, and markets in Philadelphia and other cities. Goldsboro, originally known as "Old Town," was a small, prosperous town with residential buildings and several small industrial and canning operations. The town's name was changed to "Goldsborough" in about 1870 to honor Dr. G. W. Goldsborough, the owner of most of the land around the town. Eventually, the name was shortened to "Goldsboro." The station is owned by the town today, and they have hopes of restoring the property.

The "Strawberry Capital of the World" is a title several cities claim, but Ridgley, Maryland, came by the name thanks to the railroad. The town was established on May 13, 1867, by the Maryland and Baltimore Land Association on land purchased from Thomas Bell and Reverend Greenbury W. Ridgely, whose name the town would take. Ridgely's economy flourished because of its local crop production, including strawberries, huckleberries, vegetables, eggs, and poultry. Most crops were processed in Ridgely or sent to various locations on the railroad. The railroad station houses the local historical society and has been restored to almost the exact specification used when it was constructed. (*Top: Courtesy of the Ridgely Historical Society*)

At The P. B. & W. Depot,
Easton, Md.

Already the county seat long before the railroad came calling, Easton, Maryland, was already a prosperous agricultural setting when the first station was built in 1876. The station would eventually also play host to the Baltimore, Chesapeake, and Atlantic Railway when it came to Easton in 1886, after that line had originally constructed its own station; however, the main station would serve both lines. By the late 1970s, the station sat in need of major repair. The rails were removed, a "Rails to Trails" path was installed, and the building was restored by the city of Easton. Today, it houses governmental offices with interpretive signs about the station, detailing the history of the railroad. (*Top: Courtesy of the Talbot Historical Society*)

Earning its name from either wolf traps or a Trappist monastery, Trappe, Maryland, has been debated for decades because most say the town never was a stop on the railroad. Well, that is not entirely true. Actually, a very large station was constructed around the year 1870 by the Maryland and Delaware Railroad. The station was first called "Melson," and later called "Trappe Station," and was in the extreme northern edge of the Trappe district. Due to its location, the town of Trappe itself saw little impact from the railroad. Today, the former railroad station is a beautiful Tudor home, showing little exterior change from its past. (*Top: Courtesy of Keith Short and Jim Bowden*)

8

THE KENT COUNTY RAILROAD

Comprising three different sections, the first built was the Kent County Railroad in April 1870. The dream of this line was to move freight and passengers from Baltimore to New Jersey and beyond. The plans to run from Rock Hall, Maryland, to Woodland Beach, Delaware, created the line's second name in 1873 when the Smyrna and Delaware Bay Railroad purchased the line. Sold again in 1879 and renamed the Baltimore and Delaware Bay Railroad, the line never reached Rock Hall, Maryland, nor Tolchester Beach, Maryland, even though the second part was graded. The end of the line finally settled in Chestertown, Maryland. Ferry operations to New Jersey from the Woodland Beach side did occur, but a hurricane in September 1889 destroyed the dock and ended that operation. (*Courtesy of the Library of Congress, Geography and Map Division*)

Most of the stops on the Kent County Railroad line were small railroad stations, built to handle minimal passenger traffic, such as the station at Blacks, Maryland. A small cannery was constructed by a company named "Swing Brothers," and according to maps of the areas, it was in service until the mid-1920s. Never having a store or any kind of hotel in the area, the railroad constructed a bunk house at the crossing for employees to use. The station has been moved to near Chestertown, Maryland, but it sits empty today.

Kennedyville, Maryland, was already a small community in Kent County and had been farmed for grain since the early eighteenth century. The area also had ties with Philadelphia's Quaker merchants and millers. Kennedyville was laid out by John Kennedy of Port Kennedy, Chester County, Pennsylvania, in the mid-nineteenth century. In 1856, the Kent County Railroad was chartered, with the intent to extend rail service eventually to Rock Hall so that oysters and farm products could be shipped by train to northern cities. Sitting vacant for several years, the station was purchased, carefully removed, reconstructed, and restored as a station on the Wilmington and Western Tourist line in Northern New Castle, Delaware.

Named for the nearby creek, Worton, Maryland, was already a small farming community when the railroad came onto the scene. Since this was to be the junction for the line running to Rock Hall, the area was expected to grow rapidly due to the amount of seafood that would pass through on its way north. A cannery, milk station, warehouse, and bunk house were all constructed along the junction. None of these plans came to pass, and the station and the town were resigned to remaining a small stop on the line. Moved in the 1940s, the station sits on private land today.

Founded in 1706, Chestertown rose in stature when it was named one of Maryland's six royal ports of entry. Named after the Chester River, by the mid-eighteenth century, Chestertown trailed only Annapolis and was considered Maryland's second leading port. These factors made the city an obvious stop for the railroad. The line continued past the station and directly to the waterfront. The station that exists today was constructed in 1902 by the Pennsylvania Railroad and today sits 44 feet north of its original location. The building retains most of its originally architecture and finer details such as the wainscoting inside the station.

9

THE DORCHESTER AND DELAWARE RAILROAD

Although the Maryland portion of this line was approved a whole year early than the Delaware section, the Dorchester and Delaware Railroad was completed first in Delaware in 1867 and it took a construction loan from the Delaware Railroad to build the Maryland section, which did not open until 1869. Connecting what was then Maryland's second largest city on the eastern shore to the main line of the Delaware Railroad at Seaford, the line quickly became profitable and stayed that way until after World War Two. This was due to the large number of seafood and agricultural goods produced in the area. (*Courtesy of the Library of Congress, Geography and Map Division*)

The railroad station at Cambridge, Maryland, was the second building at this location. Constructed in 1901 to replace the smaller old station, the building was one of the largest railroad stations constructed on Delmarva. The need for a new station was due to the true boom of Cambridge. Within twenty years of the railroad's arrival, the town had quintupled in size. The Phillips Packing Company, the area's largest employer in the early 1900s, employed no fewer than 10,000 people. The station became a bus stop in the 1970s and today has been restored and serves as a real estate office. (*Top: Courtesy of John Stroup*)

When the Dorchester and Delaware Railroad was in the planning stages, it was initially proposed to run through the middle of East New Market, Maryland. Due to the influence of a large stockholder in the line who wished to prevent the road from running through his farm, the line was built south of the town. Located about 12 miles from Cambridge, East New Market was described as a thriving village with some of the best farmland in the county. Agricultural products of the area included peaches, berries, melons, and other fruits and vegetables. Today, the station sits empty, having been moved for roadway construction.

Williamsburg, Maryland, had its first small-frame station erected in around 1870. The new Williamsburg station, erected in around 1910, was a larger, better-lit building with a broad roof and wide eaves that sheltered the ticket bay as well as the area immediately surrounding the depot. After passenger service ended, the station was moved and used as a machine shop. During the late 1990s, the station was acquired by the town of Hurlock and moved to a new site along the old right-of-way of the Cambridge and Seaford Railroad. It was converted into a meeting place and site of historic interest to commemorate the important role railroading has had in Hurlock.

Federalsburg, Maryland, was already a ship-building town with a thriving economy when the railroad came. The railroad's arrival only boosted the community with fourteen canneries and other endeavors created. When the final system plan that Conrail used to decide what lines would be abandoned included this line, politicians from the states of Maryland and Delaware needed a "designated operator." In August 1977, the Maryland and Delaware Railroad Company was created. Soon after its organization, the firm was selected as the "designated operator" of the line and chose the old railroad station as its headquarters; it stills functions in the capacity today.

10

THE WILMINGTON AND WESTERN RAILROAD

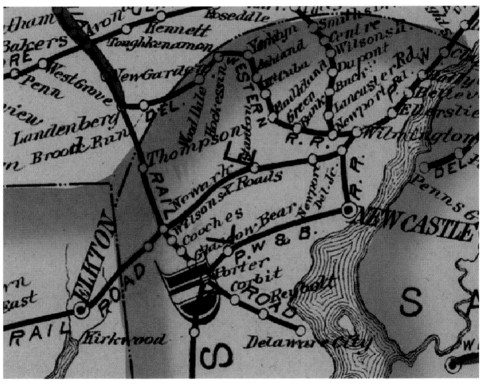

Only ever having 20 miles of track, the Wilmington and Western Railroad had a slow start. The line had already undergone three name changes by the time the line opened on October 19, 1872. The line continued to have financial struggles, eventually being purchased by the Baltimore and Ohio Railroad on February 1, 1883. Connecting Wilmington, Delaware, with the main B&O line running from Baltimore to points north, the line stayed very active with freight until the 1970s, and for a period in the early 1900s, it was the company's most profitable line. Today, the Wilmington and Western runs again as one of the most popular excursion trains in America. (*Courtesy of the Library of Congress, Geography and Map Division*)

"It is our theory that stations should be attractive, not naked, unpainted repulsive sheds," was the policy of the Wilmington and Western Railroad. All the stations on the line were constructed to look the same. Originally in Yorklyn, Delaware, the Historic Red Clay Valley, Inc., owns the station today, and it has been moved to Greenbank, Delaware. The building is used as a part of the Wilmington and Western Excursion rail line. Surrounding the area where the station originally sat is the former National Vulcanized Fiber Plant. This area was set to be turned into a park and historical area until a recent arson fire in May 2021 destroyed most of the existing structures at the site.

11

THE BREAKWATER AND FRANKFORD RAILROAD

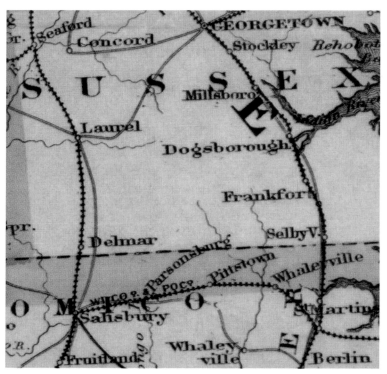

The Breakwater and Frankford Railroad started operations in 1873 and merged quickly in 1883 with other lines that it connected to in the area to create the Maryland, Delaware, and Virginia Railroad. This increased the line from less than 20 miles to a total of over 90 miles. The J&B ran through the agricultural area of eastern Delaware and allowed for the connection of the seafood ports further south to the Delaware Railroad, allowing passengers and goods to be shipped to the major cities of the northeast. Today, the line is operated by Delmarva Central Railroad and the Maryland and Delaware Railroad. (*Courtesy of the Library of Congress, Geography and Map Division*)

The origins of Millsboro, Delaware, date back to 1792, the year Elisha Dickerson dammed up the headwaters of the Indian River at the point known as Rock Hole (because of the annual spawning of rockfish there). Originally called "Millsborough," the name only applied to the area on the northeastern side of the river, where Dickerson's grist mill was located, while the growing community on the southwestern side of the river was known as "Washington" until 1837 when the two villages became a single community. The name was later shortened to "Millsboro." The railroad station today sits on its original foundation and currently is a vacant office structure. As with many towns, mills and canneries quickly spang up with the arrival of the train.

Truly founded by the building of a country store, Frankford was established in 1808, but it was not until 1848 that most people were calling it the Frankford Village. The establishment of the B&F Railroad brought a hotel, commercial establishments, and an opera house to make Frankford a thriving commercial and cultural center. The surviving building is the freight station, which was moved by Nutter D. Marvel, Sr., and was combined with the freight station from Selbyville, Delaware. Together, they reside at the Marvel Museum in Georgetown, Delaware, and serve as both a meeting place and a banquet hall.

THE DEPOT SELBYVILLE DEL.

The Breakwater and Frankford Railroad arrived in Selbyville, Delaware, in 1872. Sampson Selby was responsible for the name "Selbyville." In 1842, he began to mark packages for delivery to his country store, "Selby-Ville." The development of Selbyville accelerated in when the Breakwater and Frankford Railroad extended shipment of strawberries to the town. By 1918, Selbyville was the prime supplier of strawberries for the entire east coast. Strawberries remained a major economic base for the town into the 1930s. The railroad station was moved and remodeled in 2004 to become a local museum.

12

THE WILMINGTON AND NORTHERN RAILROAD

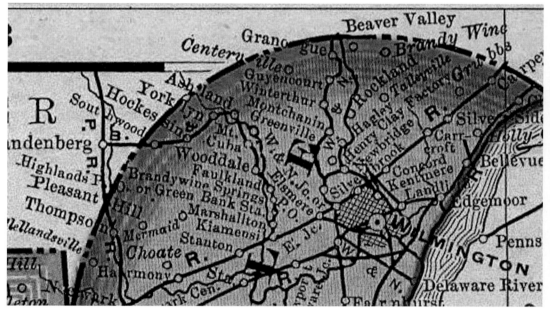

The Wilmington and Northern Railroad as with so many of the small lines on Delmarva underwent several name changes. Beginning life as the Wilmington and Brandywine Railroad, the line then merged with Berks and Chester Railroad Company of Pennsylvania on May 29, 1866, to form the Wilmington and Reading Railroad Company. The W&R was sold at foreclosure on December 4, 1876, and reorganized as the Wilmington and Northern Railroad Company under the control of its old owners on April 3, 1877. On August 10, 1898, Henry A. du Pont, who owned the controlling interest in the line and had heavily influenced its construction and route, sold the railroad to the Reading Company. (*Courtesy of the Library of Congress, Geography and Map Division*)

Beginning in 1867, railroad tracks cut across the Winterthur property, the mansion of Henry Francis du Pont. The estate was named after the Swiss city of Winterthur, the ancestral home of Jacques Antoine Bidermann, a son-in-law of Éleuthère Irénée du Pont, the founder of the du Pont family and fortune in the United States. The Wilmington and Northern Railroad used the line primarily to transport freight, although there are accounts of visitors arriving at Winterthur by train. Nearby to the station is a spur track on a bridge, likely used to unload coal for heating the mansion. Today, the estate is a museum and gardens, while the building that was used as the station is a private residence.

Montchanin, Delaware, received a post office and permanent railroad station in 1889, at which time it acquired the name "Montchanin" in honor of Anne Alexandrine de Montchanin, mother of Pierre Samuel du Pont de Nemours. Prior to that time, the village rail stop was named DuPont station in honor of the nearby Dupont Powder Works. The original settlement consisted of only 2.4 acres and was home to the employees of the surround DuPont plants. The area today is a historic district, and the old station services as an office building.

Sometimes, you just run out of names and you go with what is simple. Thus is the case with the New Bridge Railroad Station. This name came about because New Bridge station was located near "New Bridge," a covered bridge at the bottom of the road the railroad crossed over. The branch line itself was known as the "Kentmere Branch" and was constructed to again serve the DuPont and other factories in the area. The line is also host to the only railroad tunnel in Delaware. Built because of the soot the engines created, getting Mrs. Copeland's (a DuPont herself) guest clothes dirty, it sits next to the station, which is a private residence.

13

The New York, Philadelphia, and Norfolk Railroad

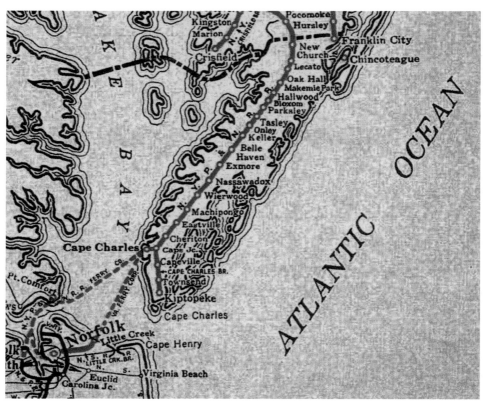

The New York, Philadelphia, and Norfolk Railroad was built from the idea that coal needed a cheaper and faster way to reach the south. It was William Lawrence Scott, a Pennsylvania coal magnate, that came up with the idea to build this shorter route. He needed someone that could bring his vision to live. Enter Alexander J. Cassatt, at the time vice president of the Pennsylvania Railroad, who took a leave of absence and joined in what some viewed an impossible task. Together, they created a line that opened vast agricultural and riches, as well as moving coal along the Delmarva Peninsula. (*Courtesy of the Library of Congress, Geography and Map Division*)

Originally called Stevens Landing and located on the south bank of the Pocomoke River, Pocomoke City, whose name comes from the American Indian name of the river, meaning "black water," was incorporated in 1878. The first station constructed here, as so many were on the N.Y.P.&N. Railroad, was a two-story structure, the second floor designed as a home for the station master. The second railroad station was built in 1912 and shows the influence of the P.R.R. Abandoned after passenger service ceased in the 1950s, the station was nearly destroyed by fire in 1989. Restored by the city, the railroad station is now being converted into a museum by the Pocomoke Area Train Club.

The saying "All Roads Lead to Rome" was literally true in the days of the Roman Empire, when all the empire's roads radiated out from Rome. This became true with each small town built, because wherever the N.Y.P.&N. Railroad built a station, a town sprang from the soil. The roads on the lower Delmarva Peninsula ran east and west, bay to ocean, but within just a few years of the station's construction, it was more of a spider web—all roads leading to the railroad. Hallwood, Virginia, simply did not exist till the railroad. With the station came the town and industry. The small town today serves as the end of the line for the Delmarva Central Railroad today. The station was torn down in the late 1980s.

Bloxom, Virginia, was actually a town the railroad did not create but impacted dramatically nonetheless. The town was established in the early 1800s as a farming community. The railroad was constructed in 1884 and with that came significant growth. By the early 1890s, Bloxom had become a major produce shipping point on the eastern shore. As farm labor needs decreased in the 1930s, the population of Bloxom began to decline. By 1952, the railroad had ceased passenger service and the town's high school had closed. This was the fate of almost all the boom towns of the railroad. The station sat abandoned and neglected till it was moved to the Cape Charles Museum in Virginia and was restored.

The town of Parksley, Virginia, was founded in February 1885, the year after the completion of the N.Y.P.&N. Henry R. Bennett, Samuel T. Jones, and Rev. J. A. B. Wilson bought the farm and laid out the town on this site. A planned community, rare for the area, grew rapidly. At first, a larger station again was built, then replaced in 1904 by a smaller railroad station. Once passenger service ended, the second station was moved as well. The railroad station that sits as a museum is from nearby Hopeton, Virginia, and is almost identical to the station that sat on this site. It serves as the center piece for the Eastern Shore Railway Museum. (*Top: Courtesy of the Cape Charles Historical Society*)

Originally known as "Crossroads," this area had little to draw interest. With the opening of the N.Y.P.&N., a new era and a new name sprung forth for the tiny village. The town became known as Onley, Virginia, believed to be derived from "Only," the nearby estate of former Virginia Governor Henry A. Wise. Onley became home to the produce exchange, organized by a small group of farmers in early 1900, this cooperatively sold over 35 percent of the shore's 10,000-carload crop of early potatoes, one-third of its tomatoes, half of its cabbage, and about three-quarters of its onions and strawberries, turning the area into a multi-million-dollar industry. The freight station has been restored into a local museum.

Known as Fair Oaks, Virginia, prior to being renamed Melfa, the town of Melfa was established as a result of the railroad boom happening on the eastern shore of Virginia in the early 1900s. At one time, Melfa had its own bank, sawmill, soda bottling plant, dairy farm and bottling operation, feed store, five different general and grocery stores, and a busy railroad station. From the Melfa rail station, you could do everything from travel to have furniture and mattresses shipped in via railcar. The old freight station has been relocated and preserved for future use.

The beginnings of Exmore, Virginia, are described by H. C. Davis, who went there as a railroad employee prior to the railroad's passing through and stated: "It wasn't known as anything-there was nothing there." Legend has it that Exmore got its name, "Xmore," because it was the tenth station south of the Delaware state line. Supposedly, an early railroad-man pulled into the station here, tooted his whistle, and announced "X more to go!" Exmore could have been named for Exmoor in England, which is more likely since so many of the areas around are named for places in England. The station here was destroyed in the 1980s, and later, the railroad station from Belle Haven Virginia was moved here and restored into a local history museum.

Native Americans called Delmarva home for centuries prior to the railroad. The next railroad town got its name from just such a group. The Matchipungoes were one of the larger native tribes on the eastern shore of Virginia and established several villages here. The word, now spelled as "Machipongo," means fine dust and flies and was the Algonquin name for nearby Hog Island, Virginia. The small railroad station was always a combination passenger and freight depot. Once the service halted here, the building was sold and moved the nearby community of Weirwood, Virginia, 5 miles to the north, and is currently used as a private storage building.

14

THE BALTIMORE AND EASTERN SHORE RAILROAD

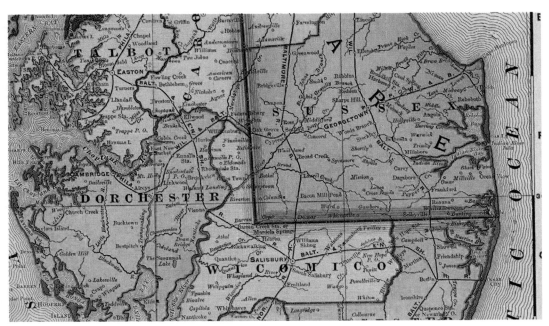

The Baltimore and Eastern Shore Railroad finally accomplished the dream of so many—a continuous railroad line from the ferry terminals on the Chesapeake Bay to the Atlantic Ocean. Beginning construction in 1889, the line also purchased the Wicomico and Pocomoke Railroad, constructed originally in 1864, which by 1879, had built the only bridge into Ocean City, Maryland, on which planks would be laid when there was no train scheduled, allowing cars to cross for a toll of one nickel. However, the line was never financially stable and was sold in 1894, creating the Baltimore, Chesapeake, and Atlantic Railway. This line would become Delmarva's first true passenger excursion railroad, with no fewer than twelve trips a day to the ocean resort. (*Courtesy of the Library of Congress, Geography and Map Division*)

Claiborne, Maryland, can trace its name back to William Claiborne, a fur trader who founded an English settlement on Kent Island in 1631. The second town in the area to have this name, the current location was first known as "Bay City" in 1886. Between 1890 and 1952, the village was a busy port for passenger and then automobile ferry service across the Chesapeake Bay, with numerous stores and motels/resorts. The area was known to back traffic up for miles to board the ferries to the western shore of Maryland. The rail service ended in 1928, but ferry service continued till 1958. Today, the railroad station sits as a part of the Chesapeake Bay Maritime Museum in St. Michaels.

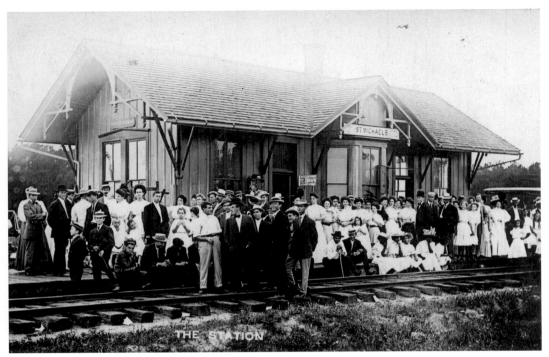

The Station

Long before the railroad came, St. Michaels, Maryland, was already a flourishing, seafaring town. In 1672, an episcopal parish was established on the banks of the Miles River and named after Saint Michael the Archangel, giving the town its name. Never more than a novelty in the community and rarely stopping to load passengers or freight, the railroad traveled the very western edge of the town. When the train did stop, it seemed the whole town would come out to celebrate. After service was stopped, the station was relocated and today is a private residence.

Royal Oak, Maryland, dates back to land grants made in 1659. Settlement in Royal Oak occurred because of its proximity to Oxford, a major shipping port. "The tree," as locals call it, is believed to be how the town got its name. It was most likely a white oak and was huge and ancient even during the time of the Revolutionary War. Someone hung cannon ball souvenirs in the tree after the engagements by the local militia. When the tree was cut down in 1867, a post was set in place and the cannonballs were hung from it. Now, they hang in the Royal Oak post office, a portion of which is the original railroad station. (*Top: Courtesy Talbot County Historical Society*)

Sometimes, we just do not know why something happened. The station at Bethlehem, Maryland, seems to fit that description. With no industry and a community at the time of under fifty people, the station seems to owe its creation due to probable needs of the railroad itself than for any other. The small station today sits about 100 feet from its original location and is a private residence. The small, unincorporated village still carries on a wonderful Christmas tradition. Begun in 1939, the post office cancels each Christmas card envelope with a special stamp depicting the wise men's search for Jesus. The small local post office stamps as many as 3,000 pieces of mail daily during the holiday season.

The town of Hebron, Maryland, was established when the Baltimore and Eastern Shore Railroad Company laid its new track through the fields of Wicomico County in 1890. Prior to the construction of the railroad, there was a scatter of houses and a steam saw mill. General Joseph B. Seth, one of the railroad's financiers, is credited with naming the new town after the biblical Hebron. The railroad helped bring in automobiles and improved farm machinery. By 1927, there were five shirt factories, a flour mill, a canning operation, a lumber mill, and a new high school under construction. Today, the station has been restored and is a local railroad museum.

Early development of Pittsville, Maryland, began in 1834 with the opening of Levin Derrickson's general store, giving the area its original name, Derrickson's Cross Roads. In 1868, the Wicomico and Pocomoke Railroad line was completed, bringing business and people to the area. Dr. Hilary R. Pitts was a general practitioner from Berlin and also served as the railroad company's president. As a gesture of thanks to his endeavor, the town was renamed Pittsville in his honor. With the construction of the railroad, strawberry farmers were able to ship thirty to forty railcars of produce per day. After the railroad closed in the 1950s, the station was moved in the 1980s and restored. Today, it houses a local business.

The beach, sun, and surf were the final destination of so many riding the train across Maryland. Due to its isolation, Ocean City was nothing more than a fishing village until the railroad and one man changed it all. In 1869, Isaac Coffin built the first beach-front cottage, the Rhode Island Inn. With the bridge completed into Ocean City one year later, the resort was born. Sadly, a hurricane in 1933 destroyed the bridge and brought passenger service via the railroad to a halt. In 2006, Ocean City constructed "Sunset Park," a small outdoor venue with a stage and restrooms. The building sits near the location of the former passenger station and was designed to mirror the structure.

15

THE QUEEN ANNE'S RAILROAD

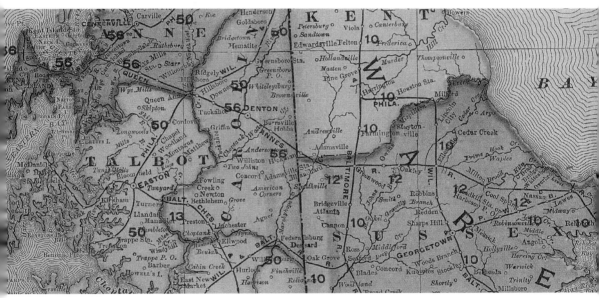

The last major new railroad built on Delmarva, the Queen Anne's Railroad, ran parallel to the Baltimore and Eastern Shore Railroad, at times less than 15 miles apart before the B&E turned southeastward. Initially, the line began in Queenstown, Maryland, but would later be extended to Love Point, Maryland, in order to shorten the ferry ride. At first, the line ended in Pilottown, Delaware, a small community connected to Lewes, Delaware. A small station even existed there briefly. The Queen Anne's would eventually extend its operations to Rehoboth, Delaware, utilizing tracks belonging to Junction and Breakwater Railroad. Through a series of acquisitions in 1905, the Queen Anne's Railroad ceased to exist and became the property of the Maryland, Delaware, and Virginia Railway Company. (*Courtesy of the Library of Congress, Geography and Map Division*)

Stevensville, Maryland, was founded in 1850 as a steamboat terminal. Farming was the major focus of the area, with farmers growing crops including corn, wheat, berries, and melons. Many of the area's inhabitants worked as watermen in the expanding seafood industry, capitalizing on the Chesapeake's supply of Maryland blue crab, rockfish, and oysters. Stevensville sits on land once called Stevens Adventure, a 1694 land grant to Francis Stevens. Passenger services stopped in 1938, and freight service ceased in 1948. The railroad station then passed through several hands as an outbuilding on farms. It was donated to the Kent Island Heritage Society and has been restored as a part of historic Stevensville. (*Top: Courtesy of the Kent Island Heritage Society*)

Rehoboth, a Hebrew word meaning "broad spaces," was initially a religious seaside resort. In 1873, Reverend Robert Paul, a Methodist minister from Wilmington, purchased over 400 acres along the Atlantic coast of Delaware just north of the Rehoboth Bay and incorporated a religious society called the "Rehoboth Beach Camp Meeting Association of the Methodist Episcopal Church." Delaware's General Assembly established a municipality for the territory, naming it Henlopen City. In 1891, it was renamed Rehoboth Beach. The boardwalk, now 1 mile long, was originally built in 1873. The railroad line was constructed right down Rehoboth Avenue. Moved and later renovated, the Rehoboth railroad station is now the home of the chamber of commerce and visitor center.

16

THE BALTIMORE AND OHIO RAILROAD

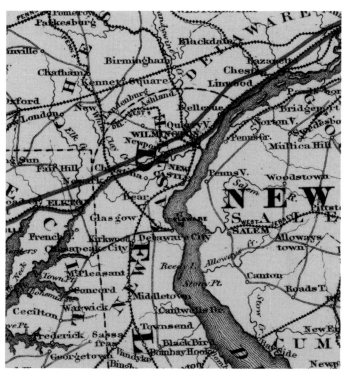

Despite being the first railroad in the United States to carry passengers, the Baltimore and Ohio Railroad was never able to establish a true foothold on the Delmarva Peninsula. After losing a bidding war in 1881 to the Pennsylvania Railroad, the B&O was informed they could no longer use the lines from Philadelphia south through Delaware by 1884. Left with no other options, the Baltimore and Philadelphia Railroad was a railroad line built by the Baltimore and Ohio Railroad (B&O) from Philadelphia, Pennsylvania, to Baltimore, Maryland. The cost of building the new route, especially the Howard Street Tunnel on the connecting Baltimore Belt Line, led to the B&O's first bankruptcy. Today, the line is used by CSX Transportation. (*Courtesy of the Library of Congress, Geography and Map Division*)

The B&O Water Street station in Wilmington, Delaware, served the Landenberg branch, formerly the Wilmington and Western Railroad, and was constructed in 1888. Frank Furness was again the architect used, as he would be on all the B&O stations in Delaware. Becoming a freight station by 1918, the building later became offices for B&O and its following iterations. After decades of neglect by its owners, the city of Wilmington purchased the building in 1993, beginning a long process of grants for stabilization, raising the building for a new foundation, and restoration. In 2000, ING bought the station from the Riverfront Development Corporation and completed restoration.

The first Baltimore and Ohio Railroad station constructed in Newark, Delaware, was located on Elkton Road, just southwest of the Deer Park Hotel. Built when the line was being laid in 1888, the track curved here and began to run a more southwest direction. The railroad station was replaced in 1945 by the building now on the site. Passenger service was discontinued in 1958. The freight-only line is now operated by CSX. The old railroad station today serves as an office.